CW01272221

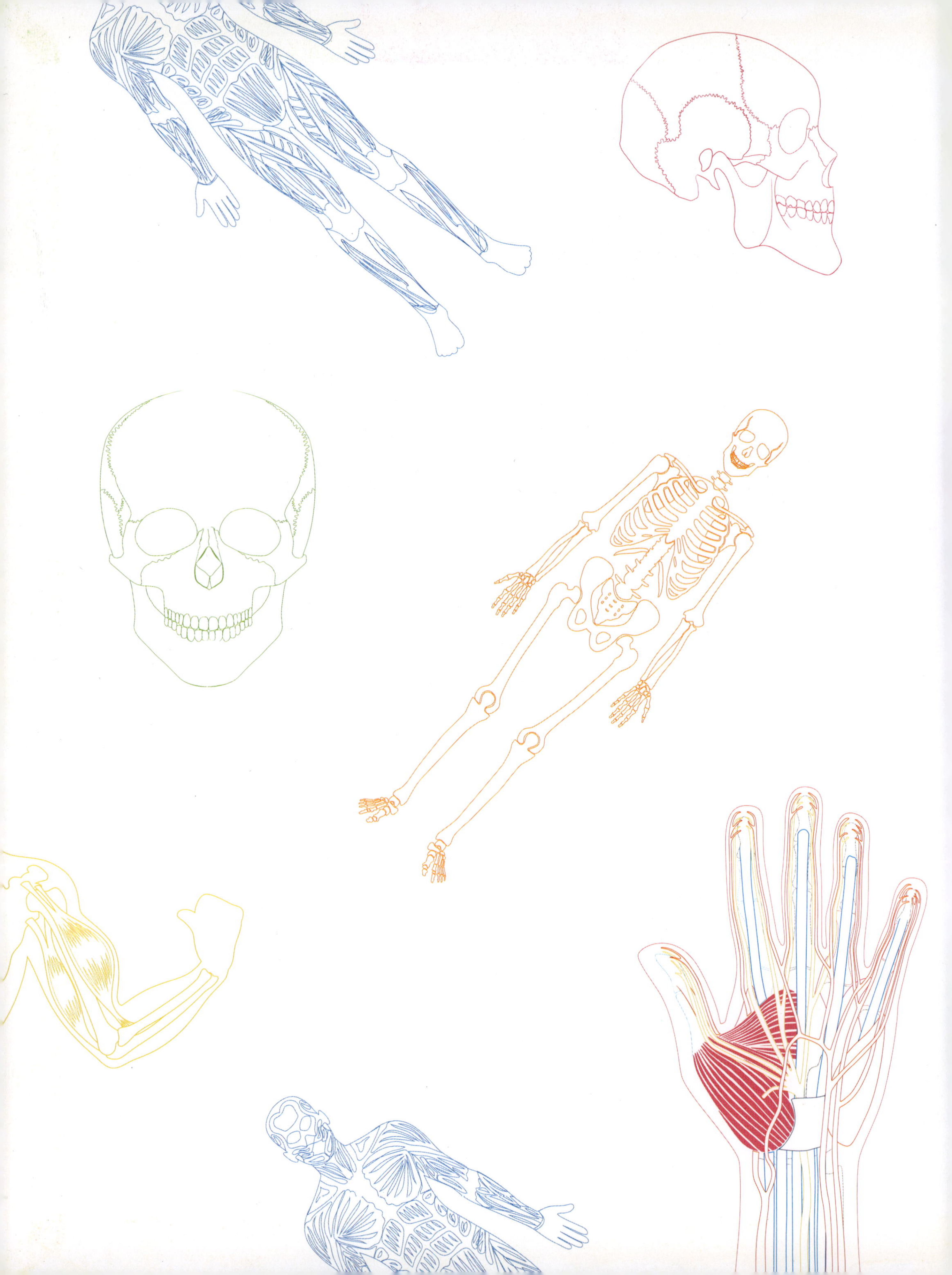

THE SKELETON AND MUSCLES

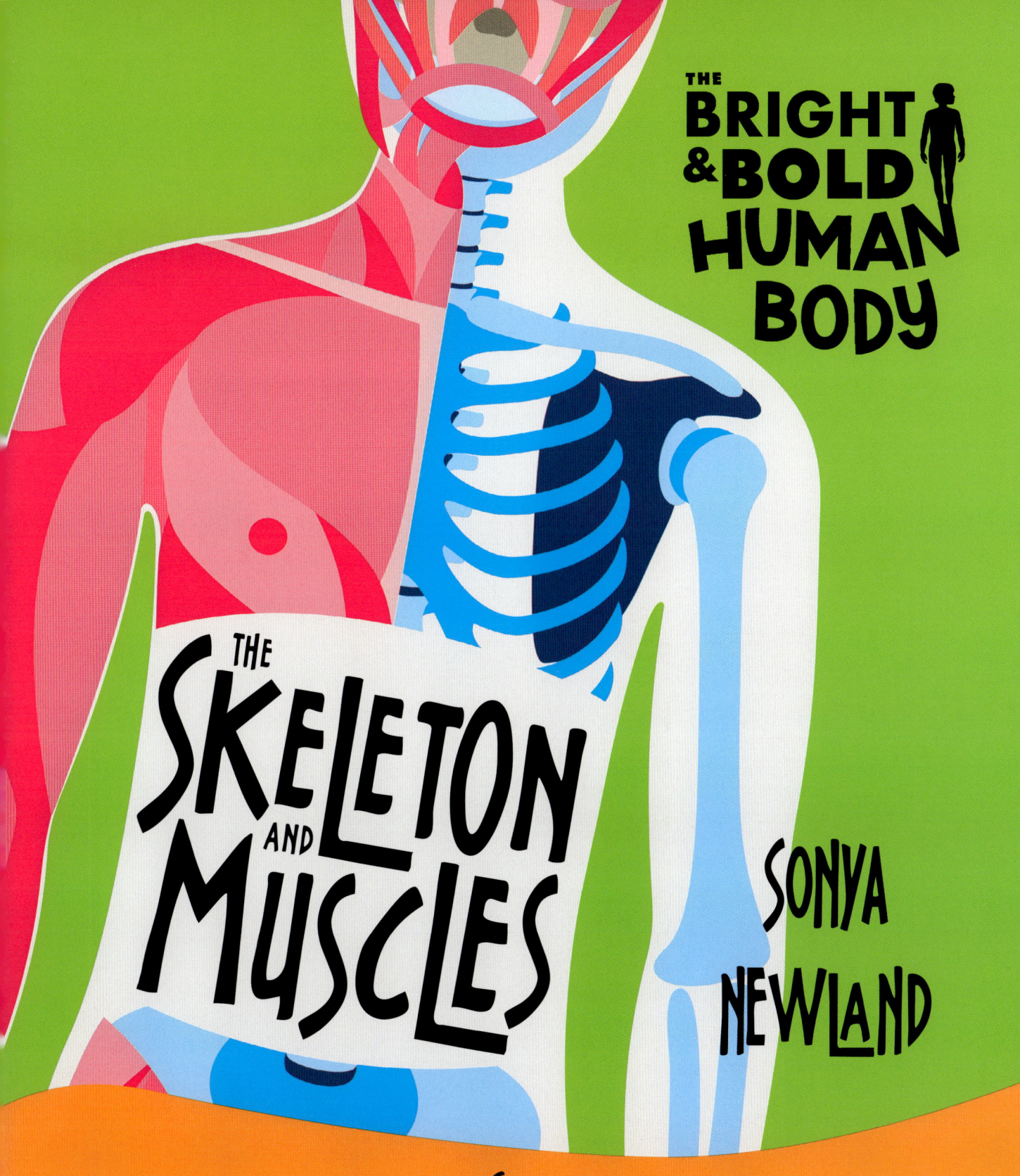

THE BRIGHT & BOLD HUMAN BODY

SONYA NEWLAND

WAYLAND
www.waylandbooks.co.uk

First published in Great Britain in 2019 by Wayland

Copyright © Hodder & Stoughton Limited, 2019

Produced for Wayland by
White-Thomson Publishing Ltd
www.wtpub.co.uk

All rights reserved.

Editor: Sonya Newland
Designer: Dan Prescott, Couper Street Type Co.
Illustrations: Techtype (p. 6)

HB ISBN: 978 1 5263 1037 8
PB ISBN: 978 1 5263 1038 5

10 9 8 7 6 5 4 3 2 1

Wayland
An imprint of Hachette Children's Group
Part of Hodder & Stoughton
Carmelite House
50 Victoria Embankment
London EC4Y 0DZ

An Hachette UK Company
www.hachette.co.uk
www.hachettechildrens.co.uk

Printed in China

Picture acknowledgements

Shutterstock: Lemberg Vector studio 4, 5l, 14m, stanga 5r, joshya 7t, Crevis 7b, NoPainNoGain 8, vetpathologist 9, Artemida-psy 10, Studio BKK 11, Udaix 12–13, 14, Ellen Bronstayn 13l, Puwadol Jaturawutthichai 13r, ellepicgrafica 14, Designua 16, 22, 23t, itsmejust 17t, elenabsl 17b, Helena Ohman 18, Bizroug 19t, VectorMine 19b, 26, Macrovector 20–21, Tinydevil 21, snapgalleria 23b, Benjamin Ordaz 24, Scalapendra 25t, Dmitry Yashkin 25b, Andrey_Popov 27, Aksanaku 28t, Luis Santos 28b, Aksanaku 29t, 29b.

All design elements from Shutterstock.

Every effort has been made to clear copyright. Should there be any inadvertent omission, please apply to the publisher for rectification.

The website addresses (URLs) included in this book were valid at the time of going to press. However, it is possible that contents or addresses may have changed since the publication of this book. No responsibility for any such changes can be accepted by either the author or the publisher.

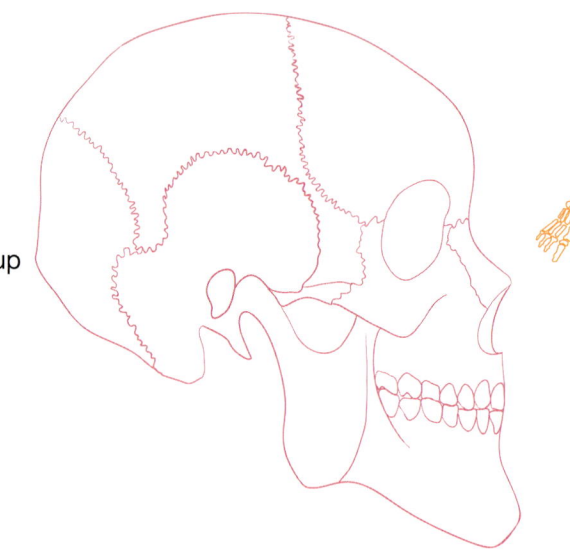

Contents

The skeleton	4
Growing bones	6
Inside bones	8
The skull and ribs	10
The spine	12
Joints	14
Bone breaks and diseases	16
Tendons and ligaments	18
The muscular system	20
Types of muscle	22
Muscles and movement	24
Facial muscles	26
Sprains and strains	28
Glossary	30
Further information	31
Index	32

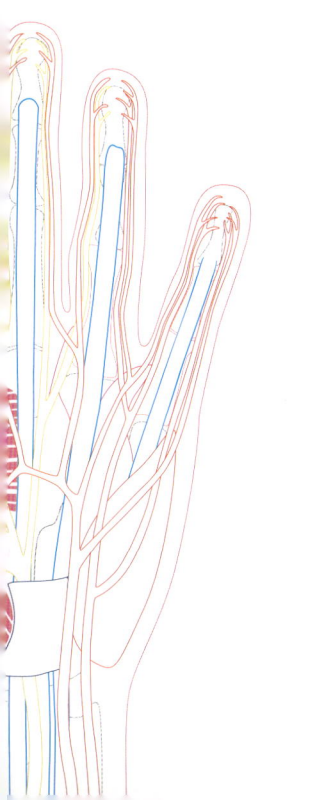

The skeleton

There are 206 bones in an adult's skeleton. Some support the body, while others protect the organs or allow you to move. Bones are also where blood is made and minerals are stored.

Long bones, such as the ones in your arms and legs, support your weight and help you move.

Other bones have irregular shapes. These include the pelvis and vertebrae.

Flat bones, such as your ribs and sternum, protect your organs.

Small, round sesamoid bones work with and protect the tendons in your hands, knees and feet.

Short bones are roughly cube-shaped. They are found in the wrists and ankles.

4

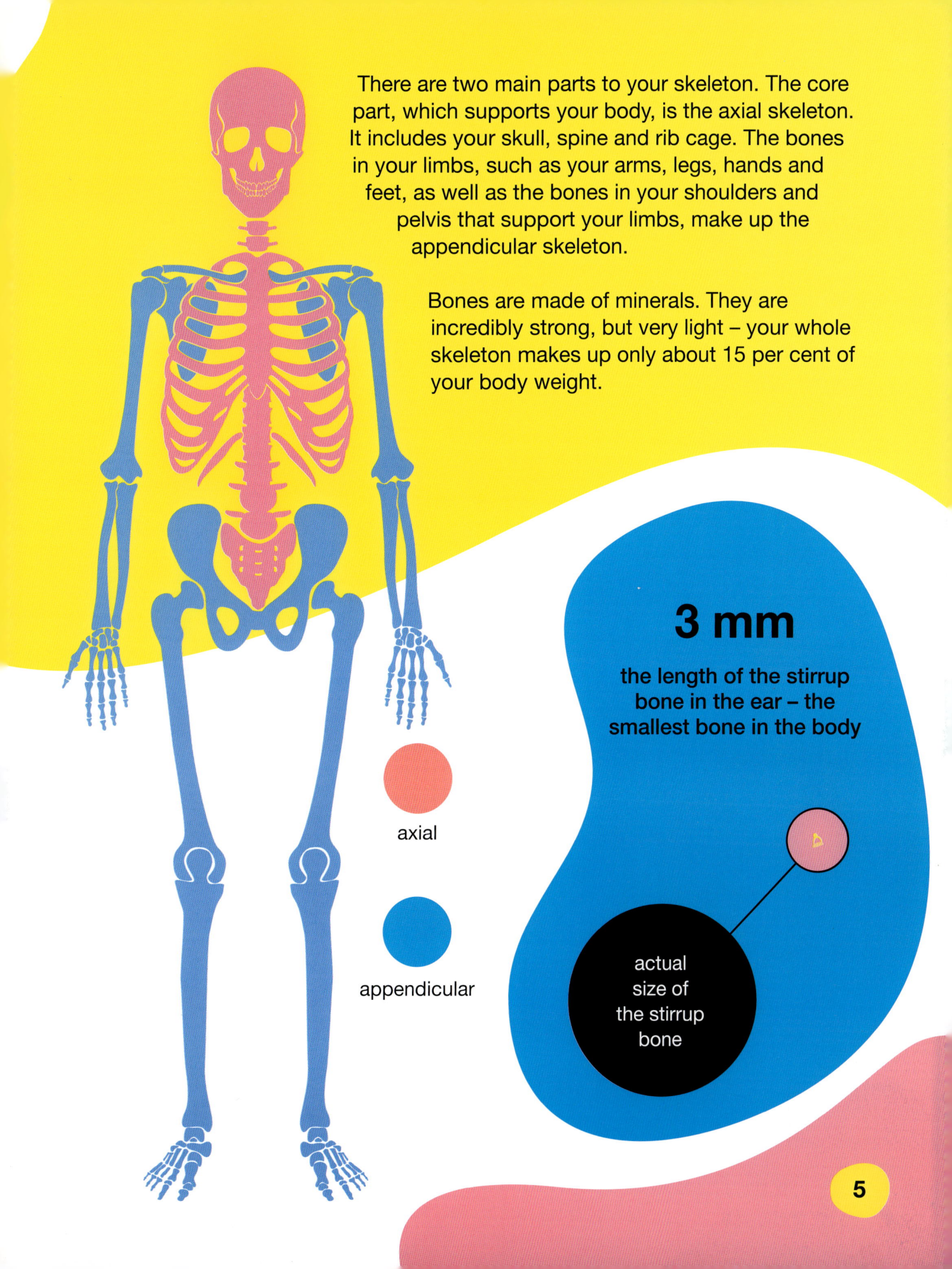

There are two main parts to your skeleton. The core part, which supports your body, is the axial skeleton. It includes your skull, spine and rib cage. The bones in your limbs, such as your arms, legs, hands and feet, as well as the bones in your shoulders and pelvis that support your limbs, make up the appendicular skeleton.

Bones are made of minerals. They are incredibly strong, but very light – your whole skeleton makes up only about 15 per cent of your body weight.

axial

appendicular

3 mm

the length of the stirrup bone in the ear – the smallest bone in the body

actual size of the stirrup bone

Growing bones

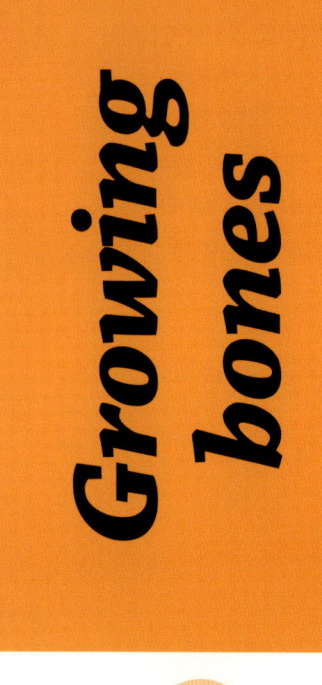

At birth, a baby has more than 300 bones. Some are made of a strong tissue called cartilage. Over time, these bones join together to get bigger, longer and stronger.

Many bones in the skull are not joined at birth. This makes the head softer so it's easier for a baby to be born.

bone

cartilage

The ears and the bottom part of the nose remain cartilage. That's why you can wobble them about.

Some bones in the arms and legs aren't fused at birth, so they can grow more easily.

Kneecaps only harden into bone at around the age of three.

6

growth plates

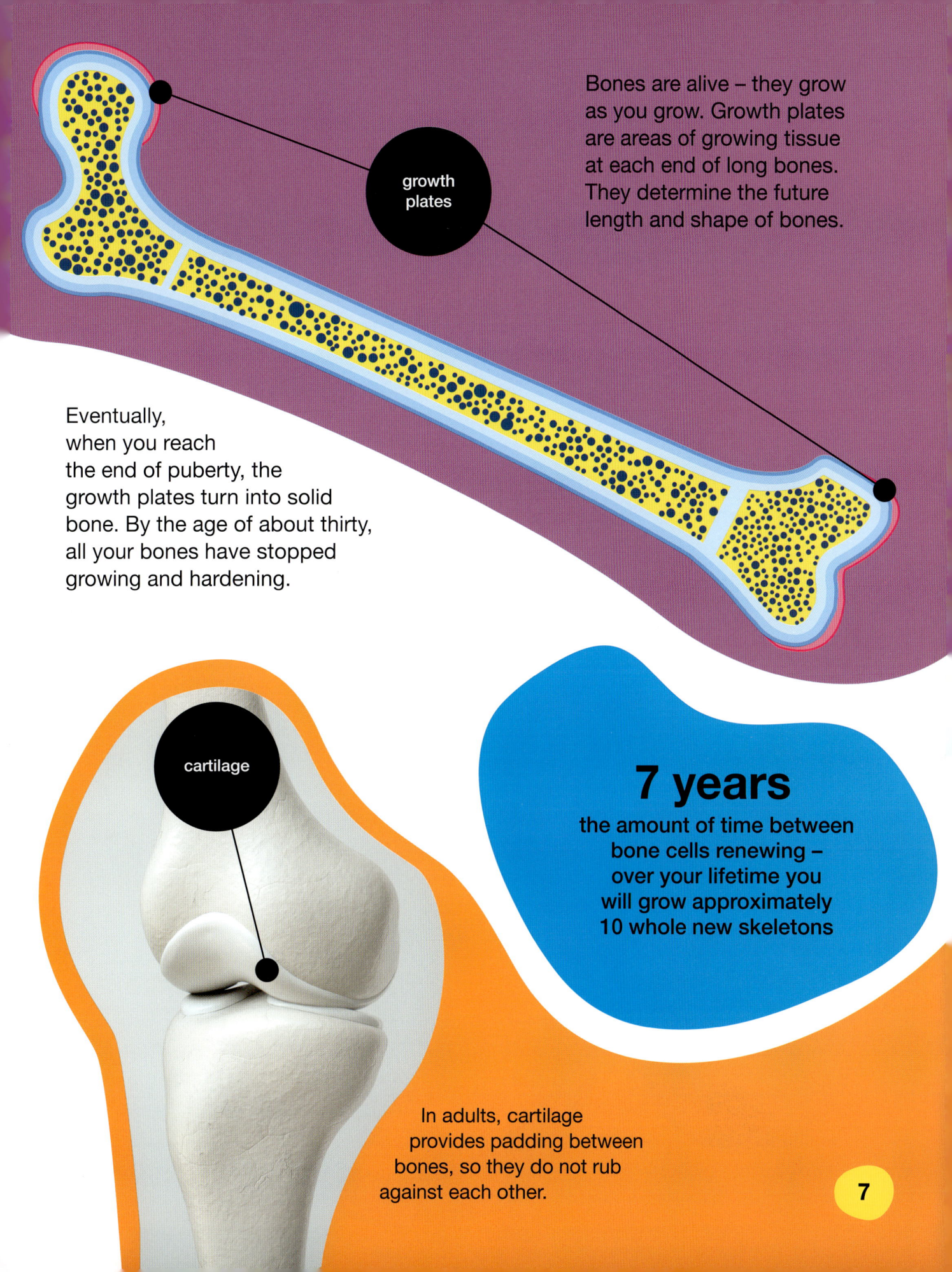

Bones are alive – they grow as you grow. Growth plates are areas of growing tissue at each end of long bones. They determine the future length and shape of bones.

Eventually, when you reach the end of puberty, the growth plates turn into solid bone. By the age of about thirty, all your bones have stopped growing and hardening.

cartilage

7 years

the amount of time between bone cells renewing – over your lifetime you will grow approximately 10 whole new skeletons

In adults, cartilage provides padding between bones, so they do not rub against each other.

Inside bones

Bones also perform the important task of making blood. This happens in the bone marrow, deep inside long bones such as the ones in your arms and legs.

The outside of the bone is covered in a thin membrane that contains veins and arteries. These carry everything your bones need to keep them healthy.

Next is a layer of smooth, hard, compact bone.

8

Yellow bone marrow, where fat is stored, runs through long bones.

Bone marrow is a soft, jelly-like substance. It is here, in the bone marrow, that adult stem cells are made. Adult stem cells can develop into different types of blood cells – red, white or platelets.

200 billion
the number of new red blood cells your bone marrow makes every day

The inside is made of spongy bone with a honeycomb structure. This makes your bones light but strong.

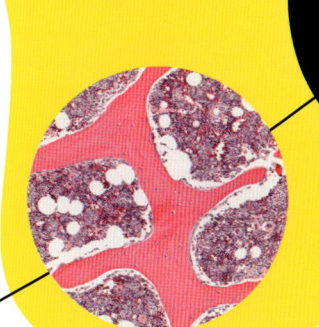

This microscope image shows bone marrow and blood cells.

Red bone marrow, where blood cells are created, fills the spaces in the spongy bone.

Different blood cells have different tasks. Red blood cells carry oxygen around your body. White blood cells fight infection. Platelets help your blood to clot, to stop you bleeding when you're hurt. All these types of blood cell are constantly dying, so they need to be replaced all the time.

The skull and ribs

Bones such as the skull and ribs are designed to protect your organs. Without this strong outer frame, important organs would be easily damaged.

The skull is made up of several bones that fit closely together. Cranial bones protect your brain. Facial bones give your face its structure.

Two parietal bones form the top and sides of the skull.

The occipital bone joins with the top of the spine.

Eye sockets hold the eyes in place.

The facial bones are at the front of the skull.

The jawbone (mandible) is the only skull bone that can move.

The temporal bones form the lower sides of the skull.

10

22

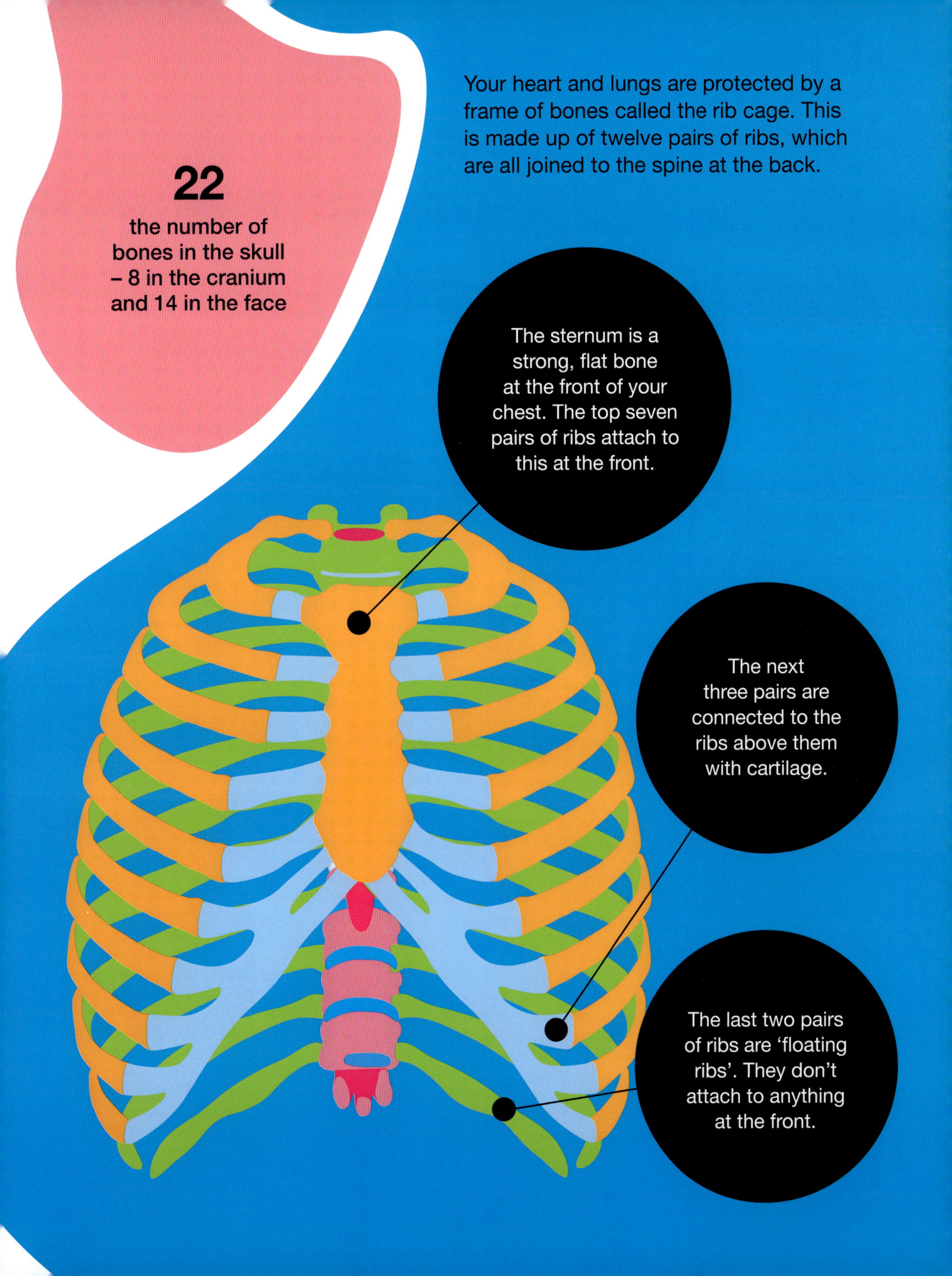

the number of bones in the skull – 8 in the cranium and 14 in the face

Your heart and lungs are protected by a frame of bones called the rib cage. This is made up of twelve pairs of ribs, which are all joined to the spine at the back.

The sternum is a strong, flat bone at the front of your chest. The top seven pairs of ribs attach to this at the front.

The next three pairs are connected to the ribs above them with cartilage.

The last two pairs of ribs are 'floating ribs'. They don't attach to anything at the front.

The spine

Below this are twelve bones called the thoracic vertebrae.

Each vertebra has a strong round body that supports most of the weight. The spinal cord runs through a hole in the middle.

The spine is a long column of bones down your back. It supports your head and body, protects your spinal cord and allows you to move.

The spine is made up of thirty-three bones, called vertebrae. Between the vertebrae are discs of strong, flexible cartilage surrounding a soft core. The discs hold the vertebrae together and act as shock absorbers.

The top seven vertebrae are in your neck and are called the cervical vertebrae.

12

hole for spinal cord

body

The spinal cord is an important part of your nervous system. It is a collection of nerves connected to other nerves around your body. Instructions on how and when to move are sent around this system.

Damage to the spine (shown in red here) can cause paralysis. If messages can't get through via the nerves, the body is unable to move.

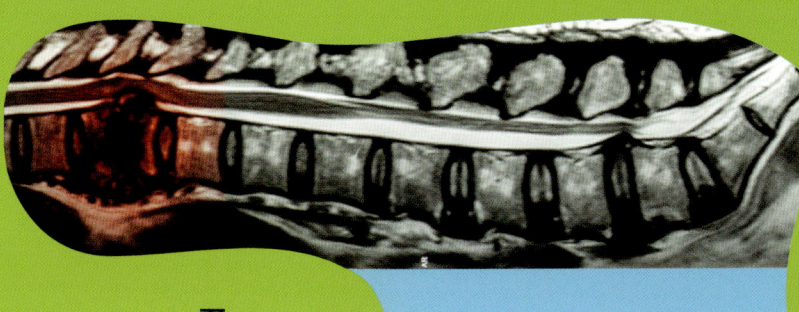

The bottom four vertebrae are fused to make the coccyx.

Five lower vertebrae make up the lumbar spine. These are bigger than the other vertebrae because they need to support more weight.

The sacrum is made up of five vertebrae fused together.

3 the number of curves in your back – these make your spine so flexible that it can form two-thirds of a perfect circle when bent

Joints

A joint is the place where two or more bones meet. There are more than 200 joints in the human body. Without them, you couldn't run, jump, swim, kick, bend or twist.

There are three types of joint:
- fibrous joints cannot move (e.g. skull joints)
- cartilaginous joints can move a little (e.g. spinal joints)
- synovial joints can move freely (e.g. arms and legs)

Different synovial joints move in different ways.

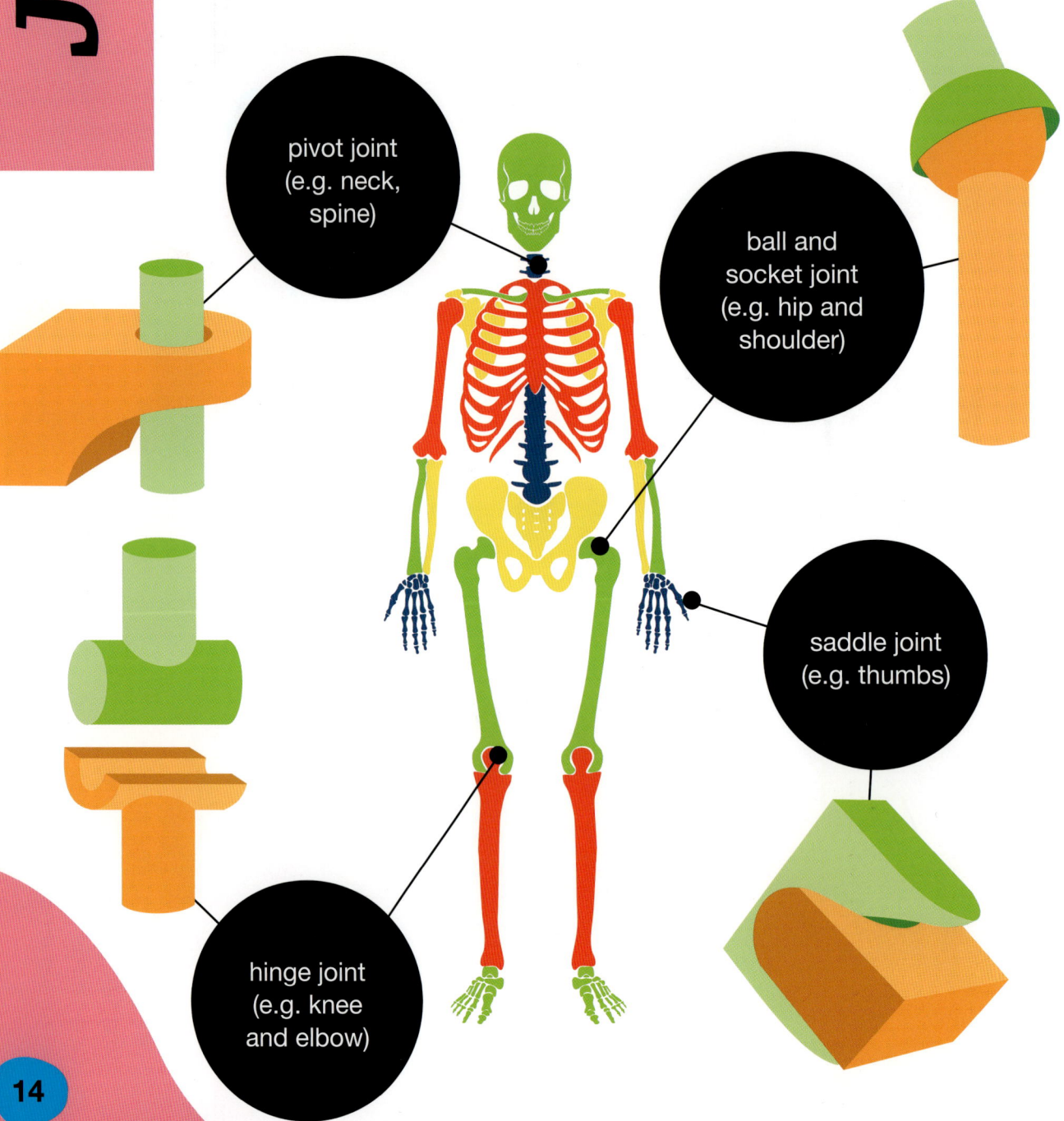

pivot joint (e.g. neck, spine)

ball and socket joint (e.g. hip and shoulder)

saddle joint (e.g. thumbs)

hinge joint (e.g. knee and elbow)

14

The knee joint is the largest and most complicated joint in the human body. It has to be strong enough to support the weight of your upper body. It helps your lower leg move and has to absorb a lot of impact.

femur (thigh bone)

A liquid called synovial fluid keeps joints moving smoothly.

The patella (knee cap) protects the knee and joins the thigh muscles to the tibia.

tibia (shin bone)

fibula (calf bone)

29

the number of major joints in the hand

Bone breaks and diseases

Although bones are very strong, they can still break. However, like almost any other body part that gets broken or damaged, bones can mend.

2
the average number of bones people break in their lives – the collarbone is the most commonly broken bone

After a few days, bone fibres and cartilage begin to form in the break of the bone.

clot

After two or three months, hard bone has formed and the break is completely healed.

soft bone

When a bone fractures (breaks), blood leaks from the blood vessels and forms a blood clot.

bone fibres

Within three weeks, soft bone begins to grow around the bone fibres.

Sometimes bones break because they are not as strong as they should be. Brittle bone disease is an illness that makes bones very fragile. People who have this disease are usually born with it. They may suffer many broken bones throughout their lives.

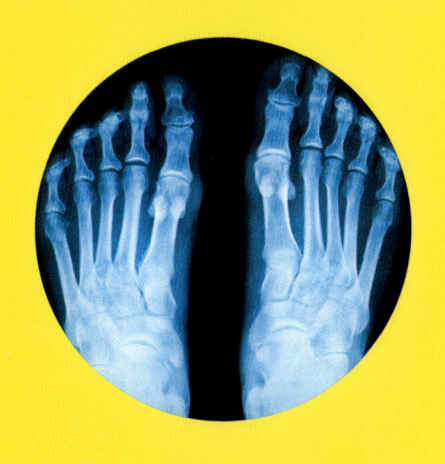

Doctors use X-rays to see inside the human body. This helps them to find broken bones.

Arthritis is a disease that causes swelling in the joints between bones. There are two different types of arthritis:

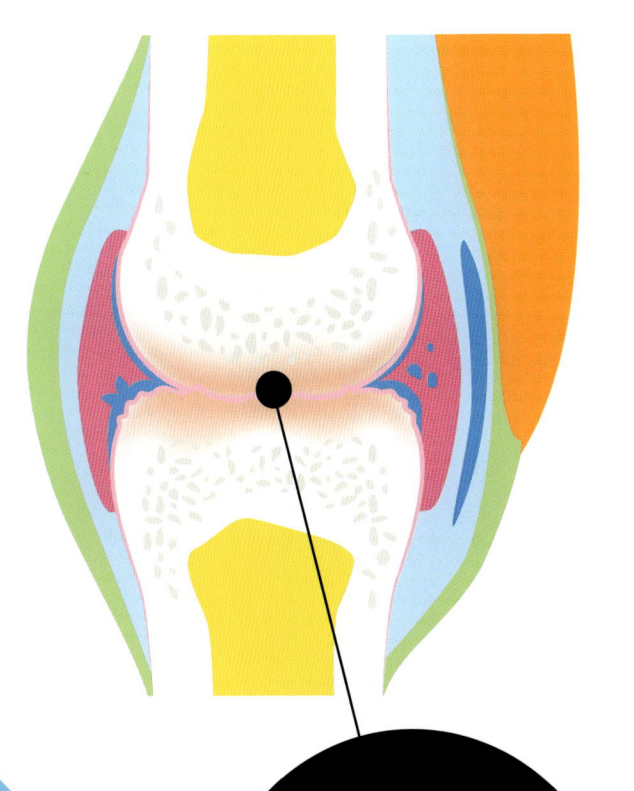

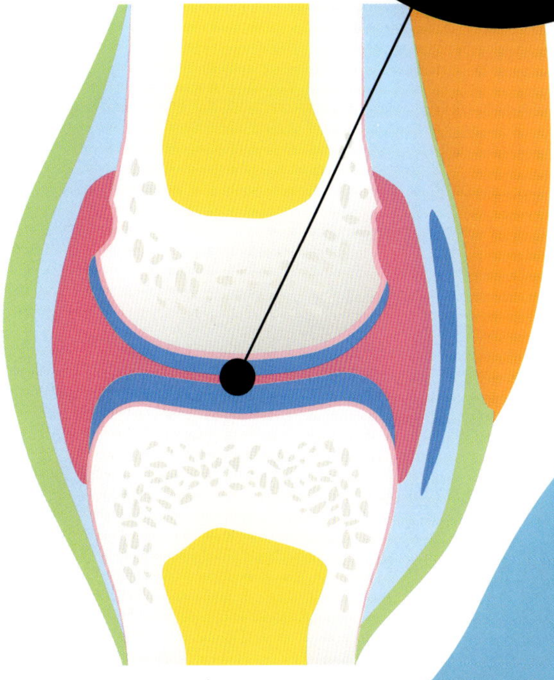

Rheumatoid arthritis is when the joints become swollen, which may cause the bone to wear away.

Osteoarthritis is when the cartilage wears down, so the bones rub together.

17

Tendons and ligaments

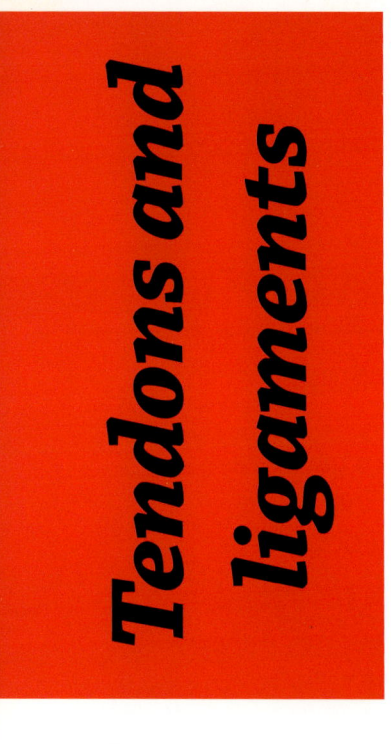

Tendons and ligaments are both types of connective tissue. Tendons connect muscles with bones to help them move. Ligaments hold the bones together in joints.

4,000
the number of tendons in the body

Tendons are like strong, rubbery ropes. When you flex a muscle, it pulls on the tendon. The tendon pulls on the bone it's attached to and makes it move.

Your fingers are incredibly strong, but they don't look muscly. That's because the muscles that control your fingers are actually in your arm. They are attached to your finger bones by long tendons.

tendon

nerve

artery

ligament

18

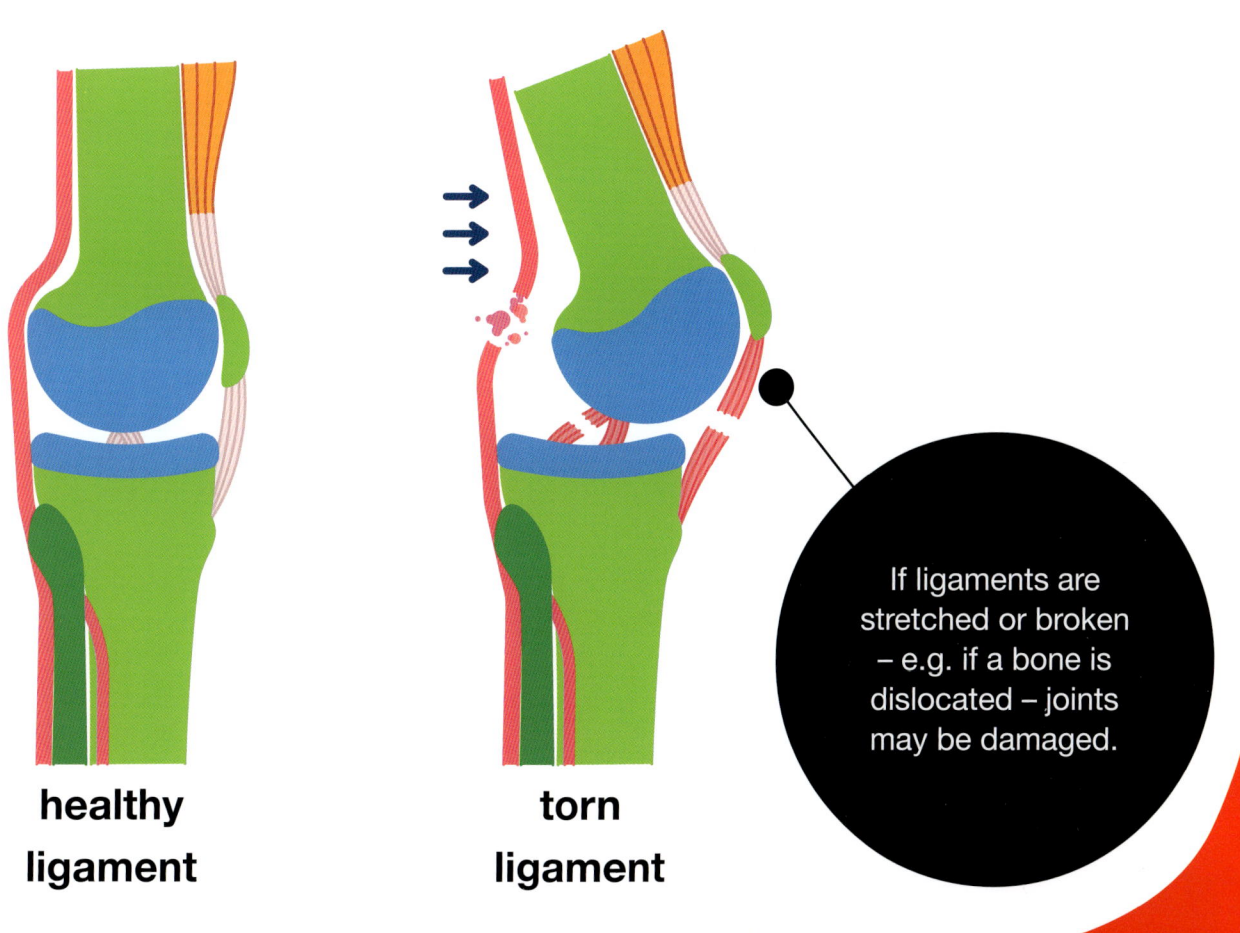

There are twenty-seven bones in your hand, held in place by ligaments.

Bones, joints, muscles and tendons all need to stay in the right place. That's where ligaments come in. These strong bands of tissue stop bones wobbling about and damaging the joints. Ligaments can move slightly, but they are not stretchy like tendons.

healthy ligament

torn ligament

If ligaments are stretched or broken – e.g. if a bone is dislocated – joints may be damaged.

The muscular system

The strongest muscle is the masseter – this is the muscle in your jaw that you use to chew.

Abdominal muscles help you breathe and support the spine muscles.

At just 1 mm long, your ear muscles are the shortest muscles in your body.

Your muscular system is made up of more than 650 muscles. All these muscles are connected to your bones, skin or other muscles.

Muscles lie beneath the skin, covering the bones in your skeleton. They control every movement in your body, from pushing open a door to pushing food through your digestive system.

The quadriceps are a group of muscles at the front and sides of the thigh. They help you do almost any activity involving your legs.

30–40%

the percentage of your body weight that is made up of your muscles

Muscles are long strands of stretchy tissue.

Muscles are made up of bundles of very fine fibres. Large muscles contain thousands of muscle fibres. Muscles also contain nerve endings. These receive messages from your brain, which instruct your muscles to work with their connected body parts to make you move.

21

Types of muscle

There are three types of muscle: skeletal, smooth and cardiac. You consciously control some of these muscles, but others are involuntary – they work without any conscious instructions from you.

Cardiac muscles are a type of thick, involuntary muscle. They are only found in the wall of your heart.

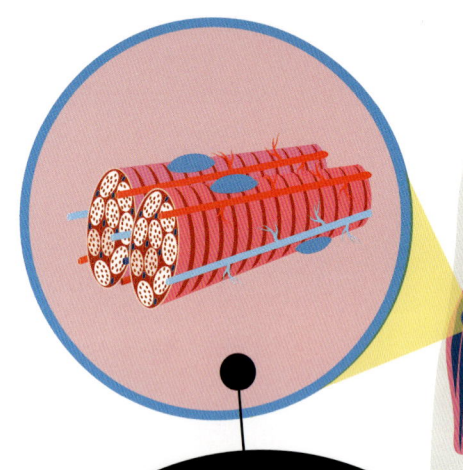

Skeletal, or voluntary, muscles are the muscles you control, such as the ones in your arms and legs (see pages 24–25). They have light and dark muscle fibres which make them look striped, or 'striated'.

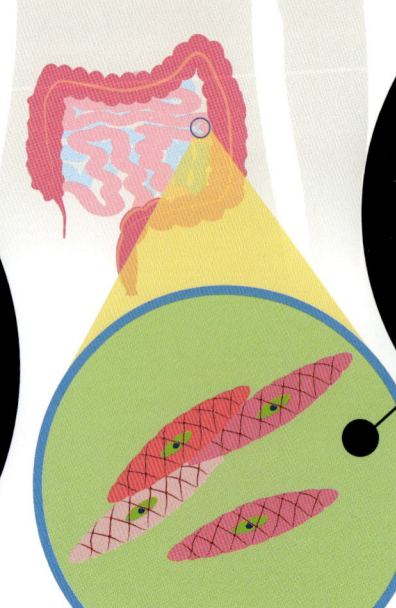

Smooth, or involuntary, muscles, like the ones in your digestive system, work without you thinking about them. They are usually in 'sheets', with one layer of muscle behind another.

Your digestive system contains a layer of smooth muscles. As these contract and relax, they help to break down food and move it through your body.

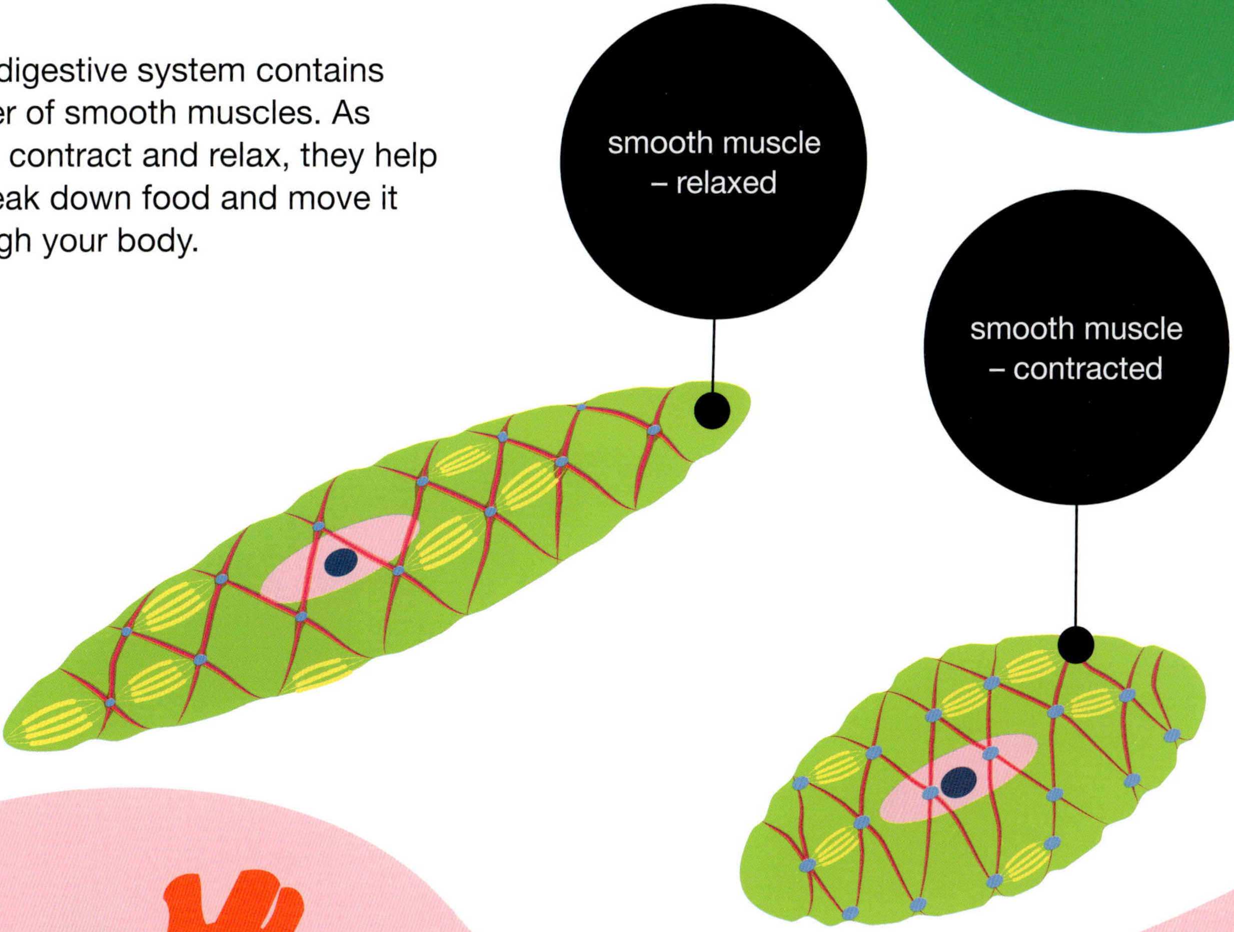

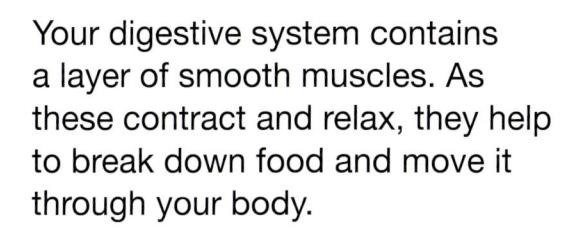

smooth muscle – relaxed

smooth muscle – contracted

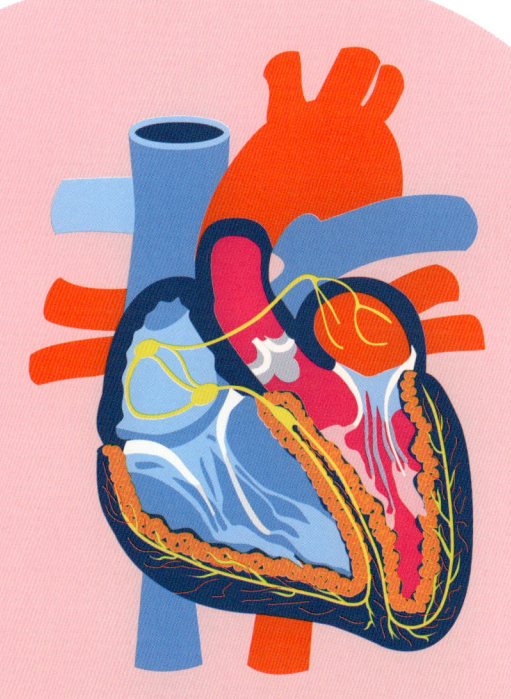

There are millions of cardiac muscle cells in your heart. They all contract at the same time, pushing blood through your heart so it can circulate through the rest of your body.

9,000 litres

the amount of blood that the muscles in your heart pump round your body in one day – that's more than 110 bathtubs of blood

Muscles and movement

Skeletal muscles work with your joints, tendons and ligaments. Together they allow you to move in many different ways.

Your brain sends instructions to your muscles through a network of nerve cells.

Movement can be as big as taking a running jump or as tiny as blinking. Even simple movements involve a lot of body parts. When you throw a ball, you are using around sixty bones, fifty joints and more than a hundred different muscles.

A muscle can only move its connected bone in one direction, so muscles work in pairs. As one muscle contracts, the other relaxes.

When the nerve cells receive these instructions, the muscles contract (get shorter). This is what makes you move.

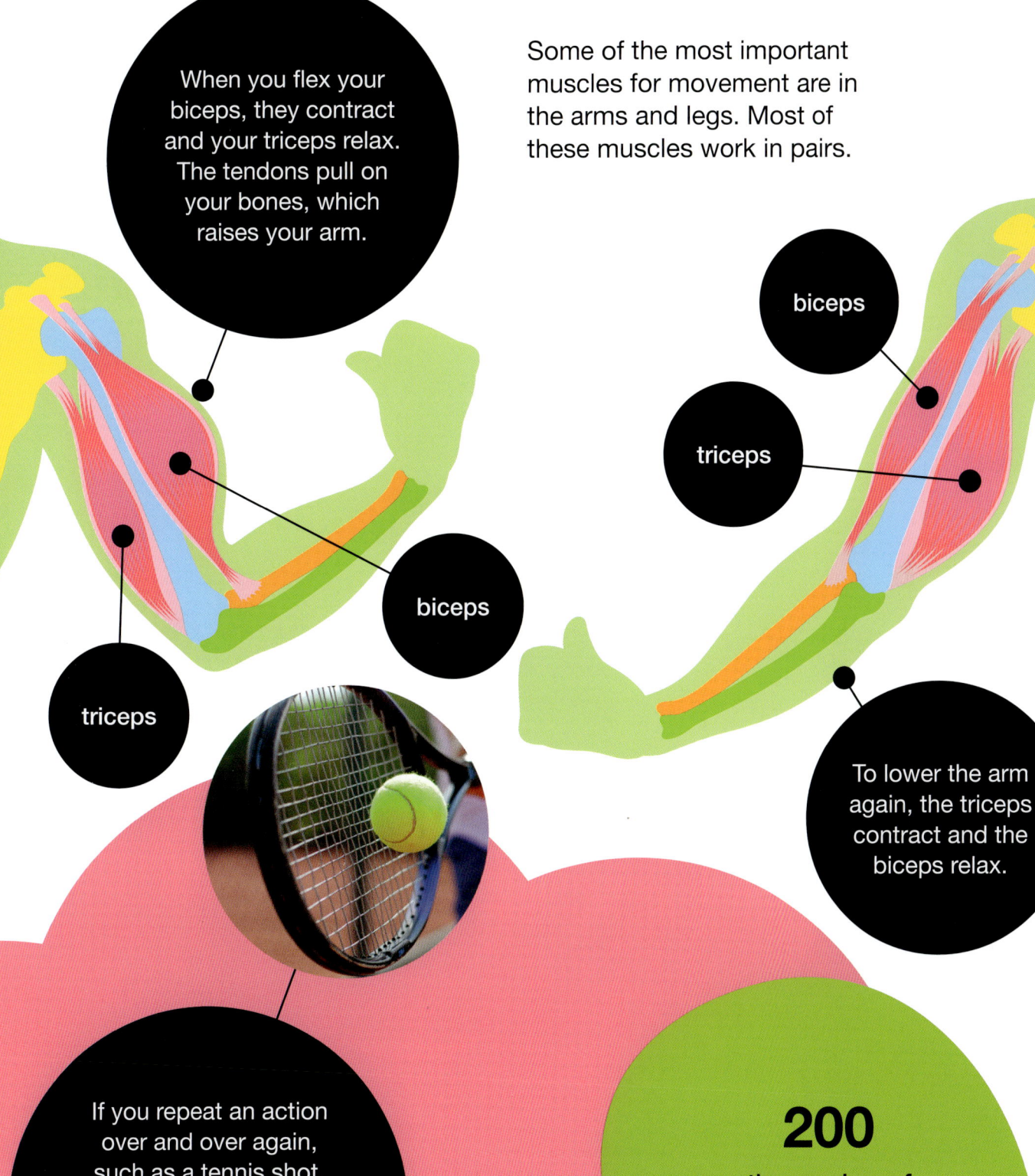

When you flex your biceps, they contract and your triceps relax. The tendons pull on your bones, which raises your arm.

Some of the most important muscles for movement are in the arms and legs. Most of these muscles work in pairs.

biceps

triceps

biceps

triceps

To lower the arm again, the triceps contract and the biceps relax.

If you repeat an action over and over again, such as a tennis shot, 'muscle memory' kicks in. This is when your muscles 'learn' how to perform that action more quickly and precisely.

200

the number of muscles you use taking a single step

Facial muscles

Think of all the different emotions you show on your face: happiness, sadness, surprise, anger, fear and many more. You can make these expressions thanks to the muscles in your face.

The procerus and corrugator supercilli are just two of forty-three muscles that you use to frown.

The temporalis muscle in your temple helps you clench your teeth and chew your food.

The orbicularis oculi are the muscles near your eyes that make you blink.

26

The muscles responsible for facial expressions are attached to your skin, not your bones. Other facial muscles help you do things such as eat, drink, suck, blow and whistle.

The tongue is an amazing group of muscles that is attached to your body at just one end. These muscles help you chew your food and talk.

You use seventeen muscles to smile, including the levator labii superioris by your nose and the risorius next to your mouth.

There are eight muscles in your tongue.

30,000

the number of times a day the muscles that control your eyelids move as you blink – that means you spend about 10% of your waking day with your eyes shut

Kissing involves thirty-four facial muscles. The most important is the orbicularis oris, which is what puckers your lips.

Sprains and strains

If you work your muscles really hard, they might ache or feel sore. Rest is usually enough to make them feel better, but sometimes more serious injuries can affect the ligaments, tendons and muscles.

The three lateral ligaments are the ones that are injured most easily in the ankle.

There are two other ligaments, higher up in the ankle.

A sprain is a stretch or a tear to a ligament. Most sprains happen to ankles, knees and wrists.

Small stretches or tears can make it difficult to move the bones around the joint.

Sprains and strains can cause pain, bruising, swelling and muscle spasms.

28

A strain is a stretch or tear to a muscle or tendon. These can happen to any part of the body, especially ones used a lot in certain sports, such as elbows or wrists in racket sports. They can make it hard to move the affected joint.

15 cm
the average length of the Achilles tendon

The Achilles tendon, from the calf to the heel, is the largest tendon in the body. This big tendon sometimes tears, making it painful and difficult to move or walk.

29

Glossary

artery – a blood vessel that carries blood from the heart to other parts of the body

biceps – the muscles at the front of the upper arm

bone marrow – the spongy centre of long bones, where blood is made

cartilage – a strong tissue between bones that stops them grinding together

cell – the smallest living part of a living thing

clot – to turn from a liquid into a solidified lump

compact – dense and closely packed together

femur – the long thigh bone, between the hip and the knee

flexible – describes something that can bend in lots of different ways

membrane – a very thin layer of tissue in the body

minerals – natural substances that help the body grow and stay healthy

organ – an important part of the body that performs a specific function, such as the heart and lungs

paralysis – a condition where someone is unable to move all or part of the body, caused by damage to the nervous system

pelvis – the large frame of bone at the bottom of the spine, which the legs are attached to

platelets – cells in the blood that clot at a wound to stop blood from escaping

spasm – a sudden, rapid involuntary movement of a muscle

sternum – a flat bone at the front of the chest

synovial fluid – a liquid that surrounds joints to help them move smoothly

triceps – the muscles at the back of the upper arm

vein – a blood vessel that carries blood to the heart from other parts of the body

vertebrae – the bones that make up the column of the spine

Further information

Books

The Skeleton and Muscles (Bodyworks) by Thomas Canavan (Franklin Watts, 2015)

The Skeleton and Muscles (Flowchart Science: The Human Body) by Louise Spilsbury and Richard Spilsbury (Raintree, 2018)

Understanding Our Skeleton (Brains, Body, Bones!) by Lucy Beevor (Raintree, 2017)

Websites

www.scienceforkidsclub.com/bones-and-skeleton.html
Explore the different parts of the skeleton on this website.

kidsbiology.com/human-biology/muscular-system
Read about the muscular system on these biology pages.

kidshealth.org/en/kids/bones.html
Find out more about your bones and how they work.

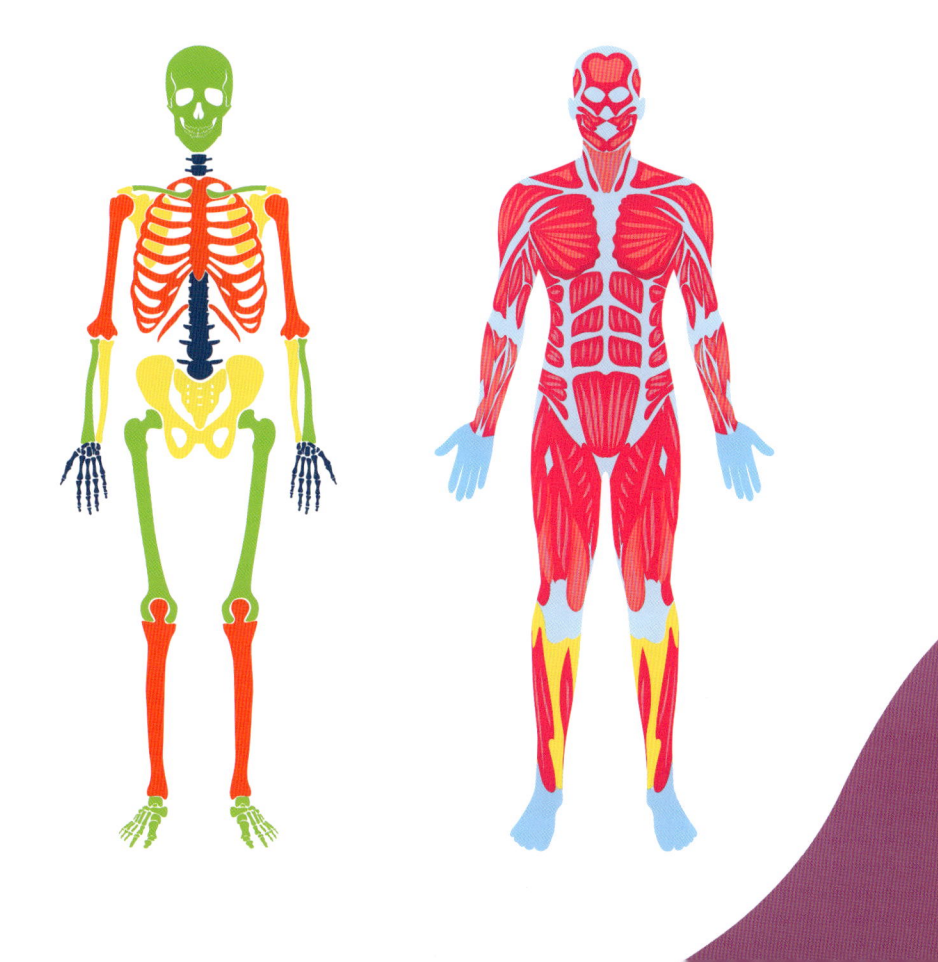

Index

ankles 4, 28
arms 5, 6, 8, 22, 25
arteries 8, 18

babies 6
biceps 25
blood 4, 8, 9, 16, 23
bone marrow 8, 9
brain 21, 23, 24
broken bones 16–17

cartilage 6, 7, 11, 12, 16, 17
collarbone 16

digestive system 22, 23
diseases 17

ears 5, 6, 20
elbows 14, 29
emotions 26
eyes 10, 26, 27

facial muscles 26–27
feet 4
fingers 18

growth plates 7

hands 4, 5, 15, 18, 19
heart 11, 22, 23

joints 14–15, 18, 19, 24, 28, 29

knees 4, 14, 15, 28

legs 5, 6, 8, 15, 22, 25
ligaments 18–19, 24, 28

minerals 4, 5
movement 20, 21, 24, 25
muscle memory 25
muscle types 22–23
muscular system 20–21

nerves 13, 20, 21, 24
nose 6, 27

organs 4, 10

paralysis 13
pelvis 4, 5
platelets 9

ribs 4, 5, 10, 11

shoulders 14
skull 5, 6, 10, 11
spinal cord 12, 13
spine 5, 11, 12–13, 14
sprains 28
stem cells 9
sternum 4, 11
strains 28, 29
synovial fluid 15

tendons 4, 18–19, 24, 28, 29
thumbs 14
tongue 27
triceps 25

veins 8
vertebrae 4, 12, 13

wrists 4, 28, 29

TITLES IN THE SERIES

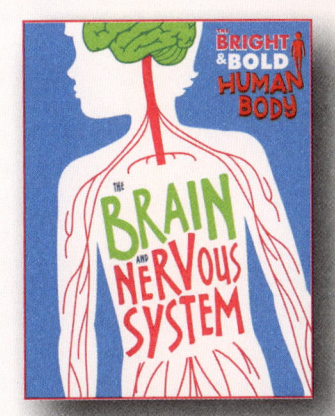

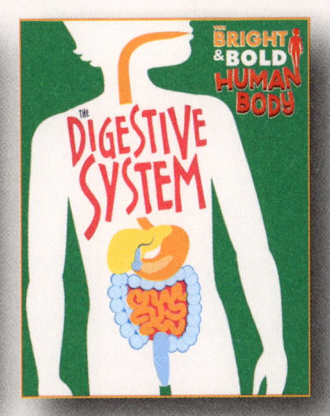

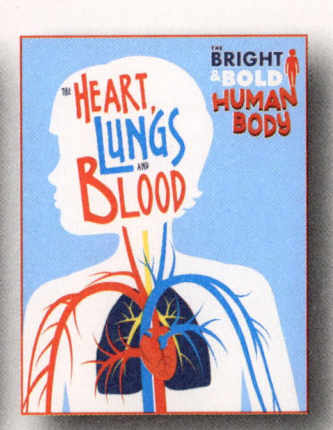

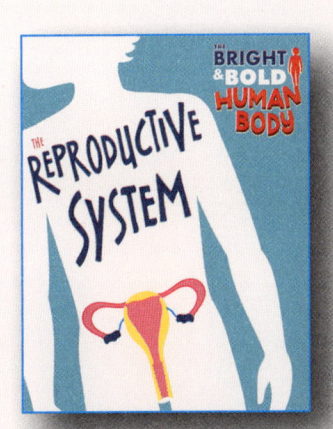

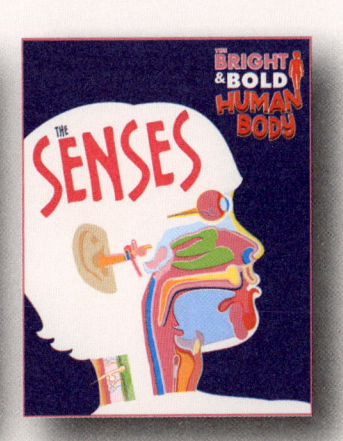

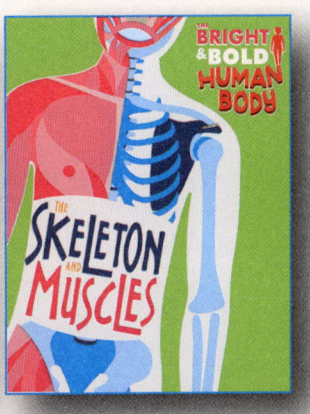

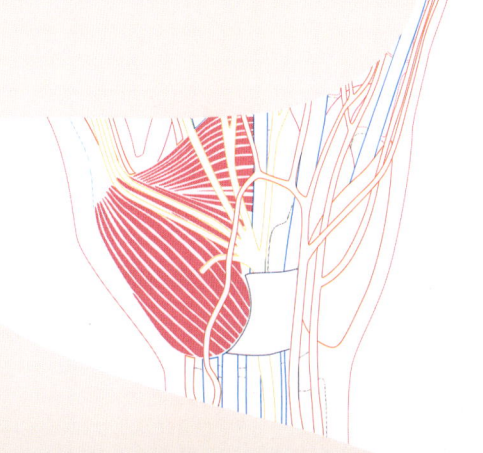

The Brain and Nervous System
9781526310408

The Digestive System
9781526310132

Heart, Lungs and Blood
9781526310415

The Reproductive System
9781526310453

The Senses
9781526310446

The Skeleton and Muscles
9781526310378

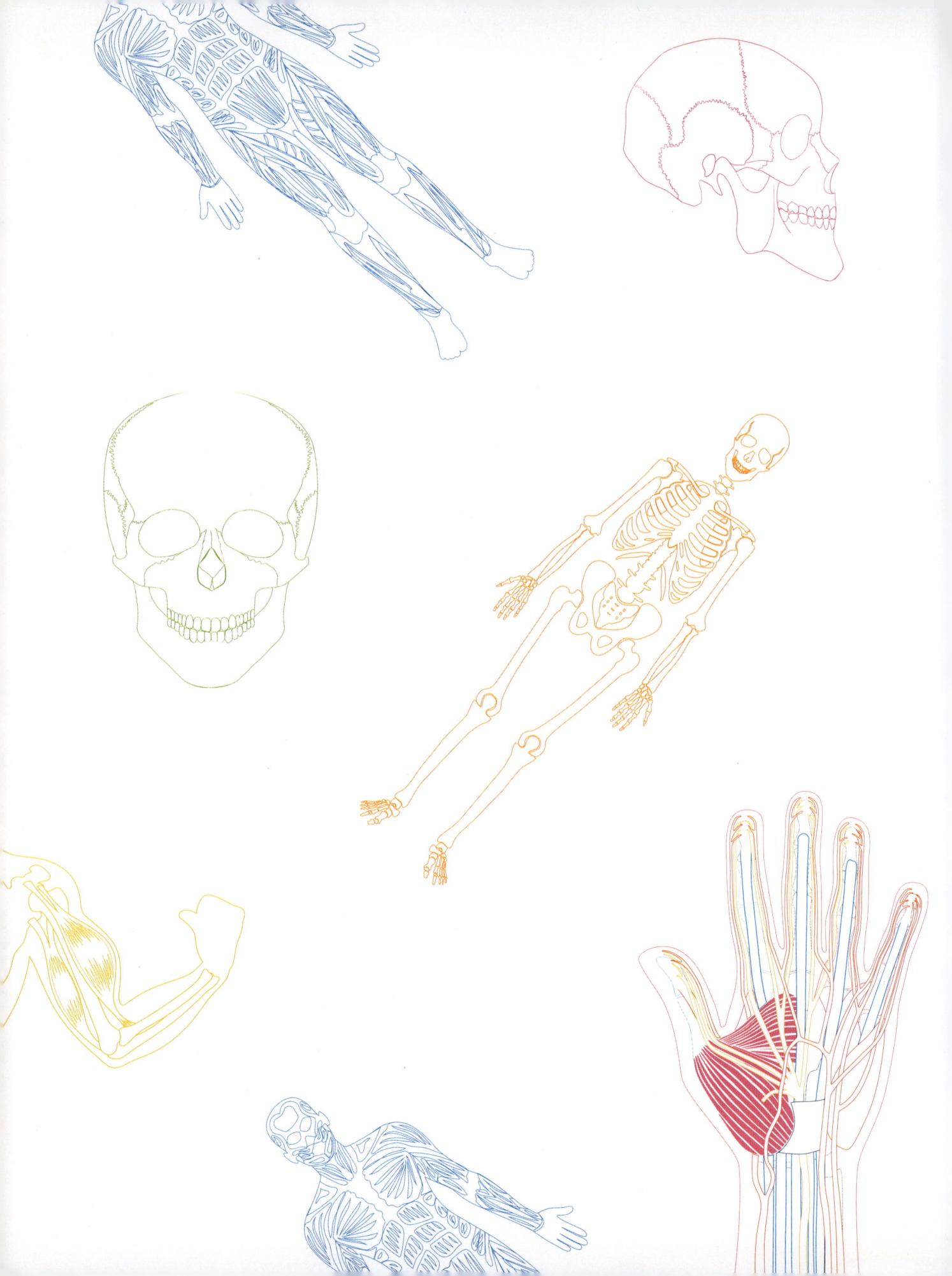